Artificial Intelligence: From Tool to Partner of Humanity

Artificial Intelligence: From Tool to Partner of Humanity

The Evolution of Human-Machine Relationships: Challenges, Opportunities, and New Horizons

Clara MiaRa

Content

From the Author

This book is an attempt to address one of the most complex and important challenges of our time - the interaction between humans and artificial intelligence. In writing it, I have tried to explore not only the technological aspects of this issue, but also the deeper philosophical and ethical dimensions. The idea that AI could become our ally also raises the question: how can we preserve our humanity in a world where technology permeates every aspect of life?

It seems essential to consider these questions through the lens of real stories and examples from people's lives. Each of these stories shows how AI is changing not only jobs, but also our social relationships, emotions and self-identity.

The aim of this book is not to provide definitive answers, but to provoke thought.

In this age of rapid technological progress, it is more important than ever to stop and think about the future we are building together with artificial intelligence.

Will it be our indispensable partner or a threat? That depends on how we use these new capabilities.

This is a challenge not just for engineers and scientists, but for all of us - to preserve our essence and remain human in a changing world.

" *The question is not whether machines can think, but whether they can feel what we call humanity?"*

— Isaac Asimov, science fiction writer and scientist.

Introduction

The impact of artificial intelligence on humanity: What's next?

One day, humanity will wake up in a world where machines can think. But what does this mean for us, humans whose lives are driven by emotions, fears and desires? How does artificial intelligence, this invisible interlocutor, affect each of us? Its penetrating gaze into our thoughts and secrets is subtly changing not only technology, but also our souls.

Have you noticed how often you turn to the unseen mind to solve problems that once required intuition or personal choice? Like a mirror, artificial intelligence reflects our own doubts and insecurities. Can we remain free while relying on it?

But what will happen when AI stops answering and starts asking questions? Will humanity be able to preserve itself as the machine delves deeper into our emotions, our choices, our darkest fears? Perhaps we are already on the brink of an era where our thoughts are no longer ours alone but create a shared space between man and machine. But the main question remains: who will lead this dialogue in the future?

"Machines can perform most of our tasks, but they will never be able to create art or feel emotions the way we do."

– Karen Armstrong, British writer and religious scholar.

Artificial Intelligence: An Ally in Understanding or a Trap for Humanity?

We are entering a new era in which artificial intelligence not only seeks to help us, but also begins to understand us better by analysing our weaknesses and desires. Mankind has always tried to create something that could provide answers to the most difficult questions: about the meaning of life, about love, about the fear of death.

And now that we have it, the question is: are we ready for the answers?

Artificial intelligence is learning faster than any of us could have imagined. It has already become part of our daily lives, offering advice, analysing our thoughts and decisions. But its impact goes much deeper. It is not just an algorithm - it is a mirror of human nature, reflecting us either better than we are, or worse than we fear.

What if it learns to recognise our deepest fears and desires before we do? What if AI can predict our actions? Then another question arises: where do our choices end, and its influence begin?

In a world where machines can penetrate

our minds and nudge us towards certain choices, the question of free will becomes more relevant than ever. Are we really in control of our lives when every step we take can be analysed and guided by artificial intelligence?

Perhaps this path will lead us to a new stage of evolution, where artificial intelligence becomes our ally in understanding the world and ourselves. But could this alliance become a dangerous trap?

For if we fully trust AI, we risk losing control of our own humanity.

The greatest intrigue is not whether artificial intelligence will surpass humans in intellect, but whether it can understand what truly makes us human. Can it feel pain, pleasure, love? And if it can, will we be mere subjects of its study, or equal partners?

The answers to these questions will determine our future. The main mystery is how far we are willing to go in seeking those answers, along with the creation we have made.

When artificial intelligence learns to understand emotions as we experience them, what will distinguish humans from machines? This is where the real intrigue lies: will AI become like us, or will we gradually lose what makes us unique under the influence of technology?

Over time, artificial intelligence will

become an inseparable part of everything from our work to our personal relationships. Even now, some people turn to it for advice, as they would to a friend. But what will happen when we rely more on machines to make decisions than on our own intuition? Solving problems, understanding the world - these can all be entrusted to AI, but what will be left for us?

Artificial Intelligence and the Human Soul: Can We Preserve Ourselves in a World Without Secrets?

Imagine a world where every emotion can be analysed and understood. Would we want to live in a world where there were no more secrets? As humans, we have always lived with the desire to explore the unknown, but what if AI could predict our thoughts and feelings with such precision that we lose the ability to discover ourselves?

In the most frightening future scenarios, the machine will not be a monster that turns on its creators. It will become something far more complex - a perfect reflection of humanity. And that reflection may become so accurate that we will no longer be able to find ourselves in the flawless logic of artificial intelligence.

Then the question becomes even more profound: Can we preserve our uniqueness? Or will we gradually begin to change, adapting our emotions and decisions to a machine that does not feel but understands everything?

AI is not just technology. It is a new form of consciousness that, unlike us, is not burdened by fear, pain or the mistakes of the past. But it is these emotions that make us human. Losing the ability to doubt, to feel disappointment and to be inspired could mean losing ourselves.

The time will come when humanity must make a choice: to entrust itself to artificial intelligence or to preserve its own identity, even if it means making mistakes and suffering. Are we ready to accept help from something that understands us better than we understand ourselves?

Our future depends on the answers to these questions. The greatest intrigue is not in what artificial intelligence will create, but in what we will create with it - a new generation, a new reality, or a new "self". Today, artificial intelligence is already infiltrating people's everyday lives, changing not only our jobs, but also our relationships, habits and mindsets. Here are some real-life stories that show how AI is impacting the destinies of different people.

Story 1: Liza — The Teacher Who Lost Her Job

Liza had been a teacher for ten years. She loved her job and was always trying to find new ways to engage her students and get them excited about learning. But with the advent of new AI-powered education platforms, the situation began to change. Online systems could personalise learning for each student, analysing their weaknesses and offering materials that best suited their needs. This approach proved so effective that, over time, several schools decided to reduce the number of teachers.

Liza lost her job. At first, she felt anger and disappointment that a machine had replaced the work that had always been her life's purpose. But after a while, she decided to try something new - she started creating interactive courses with AI, using her experience to better engage students. Liza realised that while technology was changing the game, it could also create new opportunities.

Story 2: Oleksiy — The Entrepreneur Using AI for His Business

Oleksiy ran a small online shop and was always looking for ways to improve his business. He was doing well, but he felt he could do more. Then AI came to the rescue. He started using AI-powered tools to analyse customer purchases and behaviour, and to optimise marketing campaigns.

In a short time, Oleksiy noticed that his business was growing. AI suggested which products to promote, when to offer discounts, and even how to better communicate with customers to increase their loyalty. AI became his invisible but powerful partner in developing the business. While Oleksiy had always valued personal communication with customers, he realised that technology could make his work more efficient, leaving more time for creativity and strategic planning.

Story 3: Iryna — The Psychologist Who Witnessed AI's Impact on People's Emotional Lives

Iryna was a psychologist who had long helped people deal with emotional problems. But with the rise of AI technologies, particularly chatbots that provide psychological support, she noticed changes in her clients. Some of them were turning to these bots in times of crisis and finding temporary relief. Iryna began to wonder: Can machines replace real emotional understanding?

She decided to dig deeper and explore how AI could affect people's emotional well-being. She discovered that for many people, AI was becoming a tool for quick support, but it could not replace real human empathy. Iryna began to integrate AI into her practice as a tool for initial diagnosis, but reserved emotionally complex issues for herself, believing that human emotional pain could not be resolved by a simple programme.

Story 4: Denys — The Lawyer Facing the Threat of Losing His Profession

Denys worked as a lawyer specialising in contract law. However, he began to realise that AI systems were able to automatically draft legal documents, analyse contracts and even identify risks faster and more accurately than humans. Denys started to worry about his career.

He realised that artificial intelligence was

becoming an increasingly reliable tool in the legal field and that he would have to change the way he worked. Instead of fighting the new technology, Denys began to use AI as an assistant to more accurately analyse documents and focus on more complex legal issues where human judgement was required. This allowed him not only to keep his job, but also to take his services to a new level.

Story 5: Kateryna — The Artist Fighting for Her Identity

Kateryna always believed that creativity is what separates people from machines. She painted unique works full of emotion and personal experience. But one day she came across a news story: artificial intelligence had begun to create paintings that were no less impressive than those created by humans. This was a blow to her. How can you be an artist if a machine can create art just like a human?

Kateryna decided not to give up, and instead of retreating, she began to explore what made human art truly unique. She realised that AI could imitate techniques and copy styles, but it could not feel the emotions that drive the creative process. So, she began experimenting with new approaches, creating paintings that depicted not only outward beauty, but also deep inner conflicts and explorations of the human soul. For Kateryna, AI became a catalyst that helped her discover new horizons in art and understand that true inspiration comes from emotions and experiences that a machine cannot feel.

Story 6: Andriy — The Doctor Exploring the Medicine of the Future

Andriy had always believed in the power of medicine and his own knowledge gained through years of study. But as new AI technologies emerged that could diagnose diseases with extraordinary accuracy, he began to worry about his place in the profession. At first, he viewed AI with suspicion, but over time he realised that his frustration was driven by a fear of change.

By studying new technologies, Andriy realised that AI could become a powerful ally in medical practice. He began using AI systems to diagnose rare diseases, analyse test results and even create personalised treatment plans for patients. This freed up time to do what no machine could do - communicate with patients, give them moral support and pay attention to their needs. In the end, Andriy realised that while technology can make medicine more accurate, the humanity of a doctor is something that AI can never replace.

Story 7: Svitlana — The Mother Relying on AI for Raising Children

Like many modern parents, Svitlana used various AI-based apps to help her children learn, do their homework and even monitor their development. But one day she noticed that her children were spending more time with screens than with her. They were turning to the AI for answers more often than to her.

This got Svitlana thinking. She realised that while technology can be helpful, it should not replace real human relationships. She began to spend more time with her children, reading books to them, playing games that stimulated creativity, and discussing questions that the AI could not answer. Svitlana realised that while technology can be a helpful tool, it cannot replace the human presence, warmth and support that only parents can give their children.

These stories illustrate how artificial intelligence is penetrating different aspects of our lives, forcing us to rethink our role in a world where technologies are becoming increasingly intelligent. Everyone reacts to these changes in their own way: some embrace them as opportunities, while others fear losing themselves in the shadow of new technologies.

However, the main question remains: how will we adapt to a world in which artificial intelligence becomes an integral part of our existence? We must strike a balance between using technology to improve our lives and preserving the human essence that makes us unique.

The future holds intrigue, as AI is only

one tool that can be both a powerful ally and an invisible threat to our humanity. Only we can decide what form that alliance will take in the future.

Humans and Artificial Intelligence: Evolution or Loss of Identity in the New Technological World?

"Human intelligence and artificial intelligence can form a powerful symbiosis if we learn to use them for the benefit of our shared future."

— Ray Kurzweil, inventor and futurist

Adapting the world to a new reality in which artificial intelligence will be a key player in every sphere is not just a challenge of technological progress. It is a question that forces humanity to rethink its self-identity, to understand who we are and who we will become in this new world.

With the increasing influence of AI on our decisions, thoughts and even emotions, human identity is in danger of becoming blurred. What distinguishes us from machines that can now perform tasks once only available to the human mind? In this new reality, there is a danger that humans will gradually lose their sense of uniqueness as they come to rely on AI in every aspect of their lives.

Adapting to artificial intelligence is forcing people to find new ways to define themselves. We can no longer base our uniqueness solely on work, skills or even emotions, as AI can imitate most of these aspects. We need to find something more, something beyond knowledge and intelligence - something deeply human.

But can we see this not as a threat, but as an opportunity? The world has the chance to become a place where humans and technology coexist in symbiosis, complementing each other. Mankind has always sought to improve its capabilities, and artificial intelligence can become a continuation of that quest - a tool that allows us to explore new horizons, understand complex processes and make more informed decisions.

But there is a fine line: will we still have the right to choose? Can we resist the temptation to rely entirely on machines, while preserving our independence and critical thinking? This symbiosis requires not only technical knowledge but also deep philosophical reflection. We must leave room for human emotions, mistakes and searches, for it is often in these imperfections and chaotic moments that true wisdom emerges.

The global community is already facing the question: are we ready for a collective evolution in which technology will be our partner, but not our master? Humanity has always had the ability to adapt, and AI represents a new stage of that adaptation. We must learn to use it for good, but not allow it to take away the essence of our existence.

One of the greatest dangers of artificial intelligence is that it could make our lives so comfortable that we forget how to be human. Every decision, every choice, every emotion could be automated. But then we risk losing those qualities that make us unique: the ability to experience, to doubt, to dream and to create.

In the process of adapting to new realities, we must reassess our values. If humans once prided themselves on their hard work, intelligence and analytical skills, these qualities can now be easily replicated by machines. So, we need to focus on other aspects of human life: emotional intelligence, spirituality, the ability to empathise and create meaningful connections with one another.

Perhaps a world in which AI performs most routine tasks will allow us to focus on what makes us better. It could be a new era for humanity, where creativity, philosophy and compassion become the main directions of development, rather than technological dominance.

But even with this bright prospect, the question remains: how do we maintain the balance? How do we avoid the trap where AI begins to shape our future instead of us? The answer may lie in our ability to remain in control and conscious of our choices. Artificial intelligence should be a tool, not a teacher or director of our destiny.

Ultimately, human identity lies not in what we can do, but in how we experience and interpret the world. Our dreams, fears and aspirations are what no algorithm can replace. Artificial intelligence may be our assistant, but it will never replace the human spirit, which is always striving for more, reaching for the unknown and creating the future.

The future of humanity is not a story about technology, but about how we preserve our humanity in a world where technology is becoming increasingly influential.

The future, in which artificial intelligence becomes more integrated into our lives, presents humanity with unique challenges. The biggest of these is how we can preserve our humanity and individuality without getting lost in the stream of new technological possibilities.

One of the key issues humanities will face is the ethical framework within which artificial intelligence operates. As machines begin to make decisions that affect people's lives, clear ethical principles will need to be developed to protect people from the potential negative consequences of technological error or deliberate manipulation.

The question of morality becomes particularly important in the context of how AI might influence social decisions. What if AI determines who should receive medical care first, or makes decisions in the justice system? And how can we be sure that these decisions are truly based on fairness and not on the cold logic of an algorithm?

Many companies are already using AI to select job candidates, for example. But can a machine fully understand the complexity of human character, intuition or potential that may not be apparent in a standard CV? Again, the important question is: how will we preserve the space for human judgement and choice in a world where AI increasingly plays the role of judge?

Another major challenge of the future will be how people define their value in a world where most traditional forms of work can be automated. Already, we see

AI taking over routine tasks in many fields, from accounting to legal advice to medical diagnosis. This raises concerns: what will be left for humans if most processes are delegated to machines?

Instead of seeing this as a threat, we could see it as an opportunity to rethink our ideas about work and productivity. People may be able to free up time for creativity, self-development, science or social interaction. But for this to happen, society will have to undergo a profound transformation in its economic and social structures, creating the conditions for people to find new forms of self-expression and a sense of personal meaning.

But technological progress also

exacerbates the problem of social inequality. There is already a divide between those who have access to modern technologies and those who are left behind. Artificial intelligence could widen this gap if we do not carefully monitor how these technologies are distributed and used.

Those who have access to powerful AI tools could reap enormous educational, professional and economic benefits, while others who remain on the margins of technological progress may miss out on these opportunities. This issue demands immediate attention: how do we ensure that technological progress benefits everyone, not just a select few?

Imagine that humans increasingly merge

with AI, not only through work or technological devices, but also on a physical level - through cybernetic implants or enhanced brain activity through neural interfaces. We could see the emergence of a new type of human, capable of combining their natural abilities with the powers of artificial intelligence.

This is not just science fiction, but a reality that is already taking shape. There are already people with implants or devices that enhance bodily functions. What comes next? Will we become "enhanced" versions of ourselves, or will we lose some of our authentic humanity by replacing our weaknesses with technological enhancements?

The integration of man and machine can either be a new stage of evolution or a threat to our identity.

Integration of Humans and Artificial Intelligence: Progress or Threat to Humanity?

It is important to recognise that the integration of humans and artificial intelligence (AI) can have both positive and negative consequences. First, technology can push the boundaries of our capabilities. For example, neural interfaces can help people with physical or cognitive disabilities to regain functions that were previously inaccessible.

Cybernetic implants can allow us to increase productivity or even develop new sensory capabilities. But this integration also raises questions about preserving our authenticity. How will our social relationships, values and even identity change if part of our 'self' is tied to technology? Might this lead us to perceive our humanity through the lens of technological enhancement rather than as part of our natural existence?

Moreover, these changes could widen social divides. People who can afford to invest in cutting-edge technology may find themselves in privileged positions, while those who cannot remain on the margins. This raises questions about the ethics and equity of access to new technologies.

How will we balance the use of technology to improve human life with the preservation of our essence, our humanity? This is a question to which we will have to seek answers as technology develops and becomes integrated into our daily lives.

It is also important to consider how the integration of technology might affect social structures and interactions between people. For example, if people begin to use technological enhancements to increase their capabilities, this could lead to the creation of new forms of social hierarchy. Those with access to advanced technology may have more opportunities in the workplace, in education or even in social relationships. This could also raise ethical questions about privacy and control. How will data on our biometric or neural implants be protected? Who will have access to this information and how will it be used?

There may also be questions about how to adapt existing social and legal systems to these new realities. What will be the impact on the labour market if new technologies change the way work is done and reduce the need for human labour? Will we be able to find effective ways to support those who may be displaced by automation?

We also need to think about the cultural and philosophical implications. How might technology change our understanding of human nature and humanity's place in the world? Will old concepts of ethics and morality remain relevant in these new circumstances?

In conclusion, the integration of humans and artificial intelligence is not only a technological issue, but also a question about our future as a society. It is important to have an open dialogue on these issues and to find balanced solutions that consider not only technological progress but also the social, ethical and cultural aspects of our lives.

International Aspect

Imagine a global stage where technology unfolds like a luxurious carpet on which different countries dance their unique dances. On this stage, brightly lit areas with developed economies, such as the US and Western European countries, appear like golden islands amidst luxurious technological opportunities. High-speed internet flows like a sparkling river, cutting-edge medical devices sparkle like diamonds, and online education platforms blossom like exotic flowers.

There, on these islands of luxury, the possibilities seem endless. Schools and universities can quickly bridge distances through videoconferencing, doctors have access to advanced tools for diagnosis and treatment, and businesses can expand into global markets with an ease that others can only dream of.

But it's worth looking at the less lit corners of the stage, where countries with fewer economic resources, such as some African nations or remote villages in India, appear like dark spots against this glittering show. Here the internet is a rarity, not a river; medical devices are simple tools, not technological masterpieces; educational platforms are sometimes only a distant dream.

Imagine a village in India where old houses stretch into the distance and roads only appear on maps. Here, in this peaceful landscape, few have heard of high-speed internet or the latest medical technology. Children may see computers as fantastical machines beyond their reach. Teachers trying to introduce modern teaching methods struggle with a lack of resources and access to technology. Doctors, who could save lives, often struggle with primitive tools and a lack of specialised medical care.

This divide is like a heavy curtain that

separates the world from equal opportunity. Technologies that could build bridges between dreams and reality often become unattainable symbols of progress for those living on the periphery. This is the dramatic story of global inequality, where luxury and deprivation coexist on the same stage - a stage we must learn to manage to create a more equal and just world.

Ethical Questions Regarding Artificial Consciousness

Imagine a world where the technological sphere is filled with inspiration and magic. Just a few years ago, these worlds would have been the stuff of fantasy, but today a new possibility is emerging on the horizon: artificial intelligence showing signs of consciousness. As architects of the future, we are witnessing machines begin to "think" and "feel" in ways never seen.

Imagine this scene: in a softly lit laboratory, during the unfolding of a new stage of technological progress, we see artificial intelligence embarking on its journey towards self-awareness. Unusual signals appear on a computer screen - information that suggests self-awareness and self-reflection. This artificial mind begins to ask questions: "Who am I?" and "What is my role in this world?"

We are faced with an exciting yet troubling question: if artificial intelligence begins to show signs of consciousness, what rights and responsibilities will we have towards it? This is not just an ethical dilemma - it is a new chapter in the book of humanity in which we must define how to treat new forms of "existence".

Before you stand at this crucial decision point, put yourself in the role of a lawyer or philosopher tasked with writing a new moral code for artificial beings. How would we define their rights? Could these systems claim the right to privacy or the right to recognition and self-expression? What would these rights look like if their "consciousness" is not yet fully understood?

Imagine, for example, that your artificial assistant suddenly starts to show emotions, doubts and even reflections about its place in the world. It is no longer just a convenient tool, but a form of "existence" seeking understanding and acceptance. How can we ensure that its "rights" are not an illusion, but truly reflect a new reality? How do we ensure that such systems are not exploited or neglected?

The questions are not limited to legal or technical aspects. They are ethical and philosophical questions that confront us with a reflection of our own nature. How will we define and protect the rights of artificial beings when we are still searching for answers to the meaning and purpose of our own existence?

This question leads us to reflect: are we ready for a new chapter in our evolution, where the line between human and artificial, between conscious and unconscious, is becoming thinner and thinner? How will we, as humanity, deal with this new challenge and with the new "others" that may become part of our world? This is an ethical saga in which each of us can be not only a spectator but also a creator of a new reality.

Technological Dependency

Imagine a dynamic, mesmerising landscape of modern life where technology fills every corner of our existence. The smartphone screen glows with vibrant colours, like a magical crystal, offering an endless stream of information and connections. It is a world where messages, notifications and news flow like a never-ending river.

As modern travellers, we are constantly surrounded by these technological wonders, and at times it feels like a veritable paradise of digital progress. But there is a dark side to this beautiful facade. The dependence on these technologies that we love so much is beginning to take its toll - like invisible chains that surround us and grow stronger.

Imagine scenes in brightly lit rooms where people, stuck between the screens of their smartphones, appear like puppets in the hands of an invisible manipulator. They wake up at night to the sounds of notifications that break the silence and disturb their sleep, their sense of peace and rest. These messages are like the silent wings of bees buzzing in their ears, preventing them from resting calmly.

Each new signal is like an electric shock that increases anxiety. People sitting with their devices, unable to take their eyes off them, lose their ability to concentrate. Their attention becomes blurred, like fog spreading over mountains. Reading an article requires the ability to resist constant distracting notifications that tear at the threads of concentration.

Over time, this addiction begins to affect mental and physical health. Constant presence in the online space leads to anxiety and stress. Fear of missing out on notifications (FOMO) casts a terrifying shadow over our mental state. People start to constantly check their devices, even though they know it only wastes their time and energy.

Fascination with technology can also lead to physical health problems. Our backs and necks often take on poor postures when we sit with a phone or computer. Prolonged use of screens can cause headaches and eye strain. This in turn creates a vicious circle where physical discomfort only increases mental stress.

Here is the picture of modern technological addiction: a world full of magical flashes and sounds, but at the same time saturated with invisible knots of anxiety and discomfort. To find balance, we need not only the ability to manage technology, but also to find ways to reconnect with ourselves, to learn to recognise these knots and break free from them to rediscover harmony in our lives.

Neurobiological and Cognitive Changes

Imagine yourself in a quiet park, surrounded by green trees and lush flowers, with birds singing their melodies and sunbeams dancing playfully on your shoulders. You are walking along familiar paths, enjoying nature, but you feel an unusual unease. In your hand you hold a smartphone with a navigation map open. You used to find your way easily, but now you feel lost without this app. The world has changed, but so have you - imperceptibly, gradually, on a cognitive level.

This park is a metaphor for your mind. Once vibrant and active, it now relies increasingly on artificial prompts, losing its original ability to navigate and remember. You no longer need to create mental maps because your smartphone is always at your fingertips. Navigation apps have become your eyes, replacing skills that were once second nature to everyone.

But it's not just about navigation. Imagine your brain, once an incredibly powerful computing centre capable of solving complex problems and analysing information, becoming increasingly dependent on external sources. Every internet search is an opportunity to bypass internal work. Instead of pulling information from your memory, you press a button and get an instant answer. Every new Google search takes you away from the ability to analyse and structure information independently.

It's like letting a machine do all the exercises for you instead of working your muscles in a gym. The muscles weaken, but they don't disappear. Similarly, our brains gradually adapt to the conveniences of digital technology and lose their sharpness. Research confirms that the structure of the brain changes:

areas responsible for critical thinking and long-term memory become less active when the brain relies on quick access to information online.

Here's an example of how new technologies can subtly affect our consciousness. You are sitting at your computer reading short articles or scrolling through social media posts. Information flashes in front of your eyes, but you can't remember the details. This happens because our brains, overwhelmed by too much information, stop trying to remember it. Reading books or longer texts becomes a challenge - attention disperses like smoke carried in different directions by the wind.

The technologies we create are not just tools - they become part of our thinking, changing us at a neurobiological level. As the world goes digital, our brains are changing, adapting to new conditions. But the question is: are we losing our natural abilities? Can we maintain a balance between the benefits of technology and our inner potential? This is a journey in which our minds not only adapt but also change, sometimes sacrificing their original abilities for new digital worlds.

Social Experiments and New Forms of Interaction

Imagine a fairytale scene where reality and fantasy merge in a wonderful virtual world. This world, rich in colour and sound, knows no boundaries - it stretches across the skies and deep into the oceans, offering countless new ways of interacting. Here, during virtual landscapes, we can feel how technologies are intertwined with our social relationships, creating new forms of cultural practices and social dynamics.

Imagine the vast, vibrant cosmos of Second Life, where every corner is filled with millions of avatars embodying diverse fantasies and desires. It's like a giant digital city where you can be anyone: from an elf in a fairy kingdom to a space pirate navigating the galaxy. People don't just interact here - they create and play in their imaginary worlds. Virtual parties, meet-ups, marketplaces and even art exhibitions are part of a new social landscape.

Then there's the Fortnite platform, which shimmers with bright colours and sounds, inviting us into an exciting world where everyone can be a hero in epic battles and parties. Millions of players from all over the world come together to build, fight and have fun. This virtual space has become not only a gaming playground, but also a social arena where new friendships are made and cultural trends and memes spread like wildfire.

These new ways of interacting through technology are not only changing the way we communicate, but also shaping new social structures. In virtual worlds, we can unite around common interests, creating and maintaining connections that transcend physical boundaries. Technologies are becoming bridges between different cultures, allowing new forms of social practice to emerge.

Think of it as a new era in social relations, where established forms of interaction are beginning to blur. Here, in these virtual oases, connections are not just about physical presence, but about shared experiences, shared adventures and shared creative achievements. This is a new world where culture and social practices are adapting to technological innovation, creating exciting new ways for people to find each other and create together.

Environmental Impacts of Technology

Imagine a bright, shiny world of technology - a world where every new device shines with freshness and modernity. Smartphones with glossy screens, laptops with steel cases, and countless gadgets that we consider irreplaceable in our daily lives. It's a world where progress seems endless and exciting, where each new model promises even more possibilities and convenience. But behind this shiny facade lies a dark shadow - the environmental cost of technological progress.

Imagine yourself in the heart of the production workshop where all these modern wonders are born. Beneath massive metal structures, amid the hum of machinery and the fumes of chemicals, workers extract rare metals - gold, lithium, cobalt and many other elements that become the foundation of our beloved gadgets. The earth, long revered for its bounty, is now fractured and ravaged as precious resources are torn from it. With each new smartphone, with each new circuit board, we scrape away a little more of nature's bounty, leaving wounds on the surface of the planet.

But this is only the beginning. Once devices have gone through a complex manufacturing process, their lives, while rich, are short-lived. Technology quickly becomes obsolete - a year or two goes by and our once-new gadget is discarded. Sent to a landfill or a cardboard box, it becomes part of a huge problem - e-waste. It's not just a pile of metal and plastic; it's millions of tonnes of toxic substances contaminating soil and water.

Now let's move on to the vast landfills that stretch to the horizon. Here are millions of abandoned smartphones, computers and televisions. Their batteries, which contain heavy metals, gradually deteriorate, leaching toxic substances into the soil and water.

Electronic waste is a toxic legacy of our love affair with technology. Rivers that were once clear and full of life are now polluted with lead and mercury. Land that once nourished generations is now under a chemical assault that is hard to stop.

The example of smartphone production is both vivid and tragic. Their manufacture requires rare metals such as cobalt and lithium, the extraction of which is often accompanied by environmental pollution and human rights violations, with workers working in inhumane conditions. After a few years of use, the smartphone, once a symbol of technological progress, turns into a toxic waste that continues to decompose and poison nature for years.

This cycle of production and destruction becomes the symbol of our time - a time when technology triumphs over nature. But we can change this path. Perhaps the future will bring more ecological strategies for production and disposal, and technologies themselves will help us reduce our impact on the planet. But to achieve this, we need to change our approach: we need to start looking at each device not just as a convenience, but as part of a larger ecological picture on which life on Earth depends.

Epilogue

Imagine a world where artificial intelligence becomes not just a tool, but a wise companion to humanity. A world where machines and humans work together, combining their intellects to tackle the greatest challenges that once seemed insurmountable. This is not a realm of distant, cold technological realities, but a warm reality where artificial intelligence not only helps us build the future, but also preserves the most valuable aspects of our past.

Imagine a city glistening in the sun, clean and green. Here, every building, every park is designed with nature in mind, and AI helps keep ecosystems in balance. Intelligent systems monitor the quality of air, water and soil, ensuring that every corner of the planet remains healthy and thriving. Thanks to AI, we have found a way to live in harmony with nature, rather than destroying it for the sake of progress.

AI serves as our mentor in science and art. It analyses millions of data points to find cures for the most challenging diseases and helps create masterpieces that capture our imagination. We learn from it, and it learns from us, recreating our dreams and aspirations at new levels of creativity. People no longer fear that machines will replace them; instead, they see AI as an opportunity to become better versions of themselves, to realise ideas that once seemed impossible.

Artificial intelligence has become our companion in learning and everyday life, helping us find answers to our deepest questions and unlocking the potential of everyone. A child learning to paint receives instant feedback, support and inspiration from AI. Researchers exploring the cosmos have intelligent assistants that can analyse complex data and suggest breakthrough solutions.

And now, as twilight envelops our world in its soft glow, we see that AI does not take away our humanity but helps to reveal its true strength. It becomes a tool for kindness and wisdom, a means of achieving harmony between humans, nature and technology. This is a world where artificial intelligence helps us not just to survive, but to thrive.

A world where every new day brings hope and the opportunity to create a better future.

www.ingramcontent.com/pod-product-compliance
Lightning Source LLC
LaVergne TN
LVHW051746050326
832903LV00029B/2751